THE PUNCTUATION FIELD

THE PUNCTUATION FIELD

Elizabeth Zetlin

Black Moss Press
2011

Library and Archives Canada Cataloguing in Publication

Zetlin, Liz, 1944-
The punctuation field / Elizabeth Zetlin.

Poems.

ISBN 978-0-88753-488-1

I. Title.

PS8599.E56P86 2011 C811'.54 C2011-901311-8

layout: Jessica Minervini
cover design: Kate Hargreaves

Black Moss Press
EST. 1969

Black Moss Press is published at 2450 Byng Road, Windsor, Ontario, Canada N8W 3E8. Black Moss books are distributed in Canada and the U.S. by LitDisCo. All orders should be directed there.

Black Moss acknowledges the generous support for its publishing program from The Canada Council for the Arts and The Ontario Arts Council.

Canada Council for the Arts Conseil des Arts du Canada

ONTARIO ARTS COUNCIL
CONSEIL DES ARTS DE L'ONTARIO

Printed in Canada

for my grandchildren Keagan and Zoe
who walked the punctuation field with me,
for their parents and aunt and uncle who were married there,
and for Don, always.

Table of Contents

Field Work

Some places I return to over and over again, going deeper – a relationship made in layers over a long time.

– Andy Goldsworthy

Something happens as I walk through the bush, glide on cross-country skis or hoe rows to plant cloves of garlic.

My mind begins to empty. A phrase might rush in, or a single word. Sometimes it's an idea, that if followed, consumes a decade or more.

One such thought was the punctuation field, simultaneously evolving as a site-specific artwork, a series of poems and documentation of the evolution of the field.

As a child in the southern States, I used to lie in our back yard on my stomach, fiddling with sticks, pine needles and magnolia leaves to build whole villages, peopled with pine cones.

Six decades later, I'm still playing with the natural world. My husband and I live on twelve acres in the village of Traverston, Ontario. Eight of these are cedar and maple bush, along the Rocky Saugeen River. The rest includes the house, the garden and an abandoned hay field, too rocky for any other cultivation.

So we mowed. It took about two hours, with dueling lawnmowers, to cut the grass in the field beside my writing cabin. Probably it was on those endless pacings across the field that I got the idea of letting the grass grow untended, except for the shapes I would mow into them.

Many earth works inspired me. Joe Fafard's Field Horse, drawn with wheat, canola, alfalfa, soybeans and corn on a fifty acre field. The prehistoric Great Serpent Mound in Ohio. The Peruvian Nazca line drawings.

"You can do whatever you want with the field," my husband said, both of us knowing that meant giving up the grass badminton court. For a while, the @ symbol won over the shuttlecock, art over sport.

Deer grazed inside the parentheses. Ground hogs dug tunnels in the field and advanced to the vegetable garden. Porcupines ambled. Mosquitoes lurked in the tall grasses.

"I need the shock of touch, the resistance of place, materials and weather, the earth as my source," says artist Andy Goldsworthy. I began to trust what I was doing, not knowing exactly what that was.

But walking the field was not quite as I had imagined. As negative shapes, the marks weren't easily visible from the ground. Visitors would stand puzzled in front of the @ symbol.

The very grasses that defined the marks obscured their view. Although ladders gave a better perspective, the field seemed a failure.

Only after asking a local photographer to fly over, on his way to take aerial shots of neighbouring farmers' properties, did I see the field as I'd envisioned it.

But it wasn't practical to hire a Cessna to document the work or to show to visitors. I wanted daily visual access to the field's evolution. And less protective cover for the groundhogs, fewer mosquitoes.

The second year, I decided to go from negative to positive.

This transformation was not just a practical one, but perhaps also symbolic of a much needed change, a cognitive therapy for me, language and the land.

I sourced drought resistant plants. Miscanthus, panicum virgatum switch grass, big blue stem, and prairie cordgrass became the backbones of the marks.

The exclamation mark started as a neatly mulched bed of various ornamental grasses, from short Miscanthus sinensis Flame Grass, to tall Miscanthus Floridus Giant Silver Grass.

Towering Rudbeckia Maxima cone flowers and electric candelabra mullein created the point.

The parentheses began with rototilling in black fly season, wearing a bug jacket and gloves.

It was a long wait until the eighty clumps of prairie cordgrass blended into two arcs.

Once the grasses matured, mulching didn't seem necessary. But then goldenrod began its colonization, and I had to decide whether to let it flourish or weed it out.

As the ornamental grasses are an imposition on the field, I thought I should let the natural succession of plants take over again, even though these plants might not be indigenous.

The goldenrod is settling in, along with Queen Anne's lace and scotch thistles.

Perennial sunflowers in the shape of a question mark followed the gardeners' maxim of "sleep the first year, creep the second, leap the third."

The @ symbol retired in favour of the badminton court.

The emoticon for irony lost its bracket and morphed into a colon of Karl Foerster grass, encircled with fieldstones found at the edge of the field, probably tossed there by the first settlers to clear the land.

In the 1850's, fifty acre land grants were given on the condition that a third would be cleared and "placed under crop." The very first year on the land was usually spent in chopping and burning.

Prairie grasses have deep roots, their above/underground ratio similar to icebergs. Highly resistant to drought, they enrich poor rocky soil, store organic carbon and help maintain biodiversity.

Burning as an agricultural tool originated in Neolithic times and is still used to restore prairies.

Fire is also a way of drawing on the land.

Like a field, language is constantly changing, a mobile work with its own chronology of creation.

Returning the modulators of meaning to the land allows them to flower, self-seed, decay and regenerate.

Farmers had quit haying our field. Their machines were too big to plough, seed and harvest just one acre.

Once a field is called abandoned, that word inhabits the land.

Empty, neglected, forgotten, lonely.

I sit inside parentheses. Breathe out through my spine, out through imaginary roots that reach deep into the earth.

The fields are waiting, impatient for someone to believe in them.

The Field

The moon lying on the brain
as on the excited sea   as on
The strength of fields. Lord, let me shake
With purpose.   Wild hope can always spring
From tended strength.   Everything is in that.
That and nothing but kindness. More kindness, dear Lord
Of the renewing green.

– James Dickey, "The Strength of Fields"
The Whole Motion: Collected Poems 1945-1992

An Offering

Take the winter field
where a light snow falls
sideways, swirls, then dives
to the bright ground,
making the wind visible.
Layer upon layer until
just from accumulation
an alchemy occurs.

An open expanse of land
usually cultivated, too often
battleground, sometimes only
background, and now, dwindling
genome of northern leopard frog,
grey fox, the house sparrow.

Such a field may be left fallow
or become a place to seed,
tend, gather and return
kindness to the wild.

Measuring

I pace the field, counting footfalls along the rail fence on the east, the north end lined with maple and balsam fir. A row of wild apple and hawthorn to the south. Dense bush of eastern white cedar on the west.

The field's length and width turn out to be the same proportions as a sheet of paper. I arrange the marks on the screen. As the fonts enlarge to fit the page, they seem to take on personas.

The ampersands, such voluptous connectors, tilt at the corner of fence and maple, attaching our field to the neighbours on one side, cedar bush on the other. They are the inclusive ones.

In front of my writing cabin, the @ symbol resides, a cheerful beginning, wagging its tail, inviting conversation. Two commas, or apostrophes, raise their hairy eyebrows, offering a chance to possess or pause. They splay out, mirror images of each other, in front of the handmade cedar arbor in the centre of the field, where sons marry, family and friends gather, musicians strum and sing.

Extending from the arbor to the maple bush are the parentheses that, once transferred to the field, will be sixty feet long instead of 200 point Times New Roman. Leading from the top of the @ symbol, pointing towards the east, is a question mark that will start as a mowed path, then, years later, become a curve of perennial sunflowers called Maximillian.

As an afterthought, I'll add a colon and square bracket to create a sideways grimace, as there may be no fields left untouched by irony.

Trying Out the Marks

As though my legs are pencils,
they transfer parentheses from page to field.
My whole body glides out each flank,
curves back, composing.

Lines barely visible. White on white.
Skis disturb snow the way graphite loiters
on the surface of handmade paper.

Once spring comes, I'll spray the lines
with horticultural lime. As the grass grows,
I mow the marks, walk inside them,
each symbol tangible and growing.

Memory and anticipation connect to form
a system of paths, a way of inhabiting space,
of belonging to the history of marks,
of dwelling in the many stories of a field.

From winter to winter the deer choose
familiar routes across the field.
Their paths visible after each snow.

My species also etches a pathway of pattern,
until we're no longer sure how we got here.
We suspect revelation in the retelling.

Laying Out the Parentheses

Sun low in the sky. Frost ices the shadows cast by a mound
of cedar branches gathered from last fall's storm. A mist
comes off the ground. I douse the mound with kerosene
and toss in a match. Flames rise. Ash falls like snow
as I mix a gallon of water with a cup of horticultural lime.

I tie a kite string to a wooden stake, follow the taut arc,
and spray a curving line onto the field, starting at the arbor,
ending at the maple bush. The crackle of wet cedar echoes
in the maples. Lines curl in the air, rest on the earth.
The sky almost as bright as the cobalt blue bird box
guarded by canes of rosa rugosa.

I spray the other curved line and watch the ground turn
a powdery white. Two hawks and a pair of bluebirds
punctuate the sky. The field tilts and expands.
It is no longer empty. It never was.

Three swallows start their approach, circle, then dart
to the opening of the bluebird's box, pull back, ascend in swoops
maple-top height, dive, circle, feint another attack. The dark hole
loses its hard edges. The swallows shriek and swerve. A circle of grey
surrounds the smoldering cedar branches now only a few feet high.

The male bluebird hops onto the top of his box, sits
for a minute, looks to both sides, stares over his right wing.
His chest puffs. His gaze steadies. He shimmers off.

Hawks hang over the maples. A chalky ampersand appears
at the corner of the field. Clouds of smoke stalk the ground
like birds of prey.

Grave Sweeping Day

Qingming, the one hundred and fourth day
after the winter solstice, the fifteenth day
after spring equinox, Chinese festival
of clearness and brightness. Time
to remember one's ancestors, sweep
leaves from graves, remove weeds,
offer libation and food – burgers and fries
being very popular, along with shrimp
dumplings and cakes of red bean paste.
On this day that marks the start
of spring plowing in the north,
spring sowing in the south, families
take walks in the countryside,
tread on the greenery, light incense,
bury grandmother's ashes
to fertilize a cherry tree.
Calligraphies of kites
commemorate the sky.

My own dead have settled
onto river bottoms and fields.
I have no graves to sweep
for they lie across oceans.
Instead, I burn pinyon incense,
clip and compost the matted leaves
of last year's peonies and plant
eighty small clumps of prairie cordgrass,
forty on each side of the parentheses.

Controlled Burn

Dry stalks of cordgrass the colour of butter
spread on the greening field. There is a bit of wind
and I am afraid of catching the maple bush
on fire. So I take precautions – a bucket of sap
that never became syrup and a watering can full
of last week's rain – as if that would stop a forest fire.
I imagine I am tending language, or at least
the modulators of meaning, releasing razor tips
of new growth from the weight of the past,
raking stray words into flame, as I stand guard
inside this chamber of combustion.

I start in the middle of one arc, click the propane lighter
under the plumed seed heads and watch them flare.
The maples echo the grasses' crackle with a sound
so like rifle shot, I look for camouflage. But it is just
the putt-putt-putt engine-starting rumble of grouse,
interspersed with woodpeckers, the scutter
of wild turkeys, the flap of crows.

I rake loose grass ends into the burn, wonder
what mineral traces are released. But mainly,
I watch cumulus turn dark as burnt grass,
the smolder and dance of ash in the wind.

Spiral

I walk the plane of your receding curves
mowed into wild daisies, thistles and clover.
Accompany your turns as they tighten
into the centre, where I crouch and circle,
like a deer bedding down for the night.
It is fall and the grasses are browning,
seed heads beginning to shed.

The way out pulls me and I orbit back,
a corkscrew unscrewed from its cork.
Calm in knowing both destination and exit.
Choice not an issue, mind free to feast
on yellow ochres and fading whites
of Queen Anne's lace, hump of fieldstone,
the small hard roundness of crab apple,
the way the body leans and lurches
through this most ancient of signs.

How sunflower seeds, nautilus shells,
fingerprints, smoke and staircases all
take your shape. Going in, coming out,
tracing the primal impulse of pinecone,
horn of mountain goat, the Milky Way.

Spiral bound,
    cauliflowered,
hurricaned.
    In other words –
whorled.

Grammar Lessons

Yesterday I photographed the "grammar field" as a friend called it. I thought it odd she used the word "grammar" – the structural relationships in language, when I'm sure I had said "punctuation." The difference between a whole field of study and the small, but important tools to temper the flow of thought.

The word "grammar" took me back to soft yellow sentences on freshly washed blackboards, drying to a dark charcoal. An old woman with hair dull as chalk, grey yellowing braids circling her head, makes us diagram sentences.

The class groans. I keep my pleasure secret. However banal the sentence, I can divide thought into active and passive, identify the actor and acted upon. Naming parts of speech, I find some measure of control.

Called to the front during math period, fourth grade eyes all over me. I pick up the chalk, draw a circle, open my mouth to say "I'm circumscribing the circle" but what comes out is the word that peels back the flesh at the tip of the penis.

It doesn't matter if I know it's a gerund. Naked with a piece of chalk in my hand and all the wrong words spilling out of my mouth.

Punctuated Equilibrium

Punctuated Equilibrium – the theory that new species evolve suddenly over relatively short periods of time (a few hundred to a thousand years), followed by longer periods in which little genetic change occurs.

– Dictionary.com

O modulators of meaning,
you plead with us to slow down,
take a detour, yield
or come to a stop. Such
fidgety back seat drivers.
Clarity, your one great purpose.
Misunderstandings not really
your fault. It's us who cruise February
without snow tires,
way over the speed limit,
under the influence,
rushing through your barriers
cursing # * * !

O little buddhas of babble,
take us back to the drawing board.
Tell us what comes next
when hope won't stop
self-seeding, overtakes
the wild. Please, please
slide out from the back seat
and help us punctuate
our equilibrium.

What Was Left

What was left was like a field.
Shut your eyes, and you can feel it for miles around.
Now open them on a thin vertical path.
It might give us – what? – some flowers soon?
— John Ashbery, "What is Poetry"

Are you sitting on empty yet?
Have you combed thought out of your hair?
Put aside the need for rhyme and reason?
Can you see the Japanese boy scouts in the snow?
Feel their cold shivers up your spine?
Can you swallow yourself whole and yield
to whatever may follow down your throat?
If so, you might have found, without your shield,
what was left was like a field.

Clear. Open. Mindless.
Waiting for you to feast
on whatever is there –
burnt sienna, whisker of grass,
wind scent, stumble of stone.
A field of stretch, opening to the spell-bound.
No paths visible. Destinations disappear.
A domain, a realm, a territory, a sphere.
The field breathes, its breath confounds.
Shut your eyes and you can feel it for miles around.

You are surrounded by a humming
so intense you must lie down.
A grass blade slices your skin.
Your hands clench and close.

You start to spin. The humming
gets louder, like water pouring into the bath.
Submerged, you almost drown
inside these sounds. Eyes still shut
you hear every colour and each aftermath.
Now open them on a thin vertical path.

So thin you need to adjust your perspective.
So high you fear you might fall.
You don't want to get up but you do.
You walk this shred of land
and all else leans away,
except one teaspoonful
of light that spills onto
this space meant for
hawk and raccoon.
It might give us – what? – some flowers soon?

The Usual Suspects

I spent all morning putting a comma in and all day taking it out.
- Flaubert

’

Hey you, hanging over us
like a grenade or a kernel of truth,
I bet you’re muscular as a messenger of the gods.
Though these days you probably dodge traffic
on a ten speed, charge up stairs
to deliver whatever we can’t live without,
have forgotten or left out.
You’re quick, to the point.
You never forget what you stand in for.

But brevity is not the soul.

You change the cadence of thought,
address loss, inevitable sword
suspended by a hair above our heads.
Kind of like a poet, aren’t you?
Or a politician. You take
a lot of abuse for the job you do.
People don’t know when to use you,
when to leave you out.
When you’re there it means
something is missing.
You replace the “i” of “is.”
When we don’t use you
you become possessive,
mine not yours, wanting
to own things, unwilling to share.
So simple. But you’d be amazed
at the number of people who still
confuse the statement of being
with the act of possessing.

@

Fat little alpha
begins the spiral
of leaving home,
chases its tail into
silly mistakes, buys
a pound of blood oranges
for their beautiful blush,
tries to squeeze itself
inside a circle. Upstart
alpha puts on too much
make-up, wiggles
back and forth
from where it's at
to where it's going to.
Caged, petted,
fed nothing but strudel
and rollmops herring,
alpha won't face
her own mortality,
yearns for the ineffable,
wakes each day to begin her long
journey, thinks she could
become a sea shell, thinks
she will reach the end.

&

My buxom pretzel, twisted gift
of conjunction & connection, bum
firmly planted on the ground, you lean
into spinal twist, offering an invisible
beggar's bowl to gather riches
from house to house, not
for yourself but for others,
as you whisper "come closer, come
closer than the word *and* allows."
You beckon us to join you with
a wag of your tail, promises
of always together.

Until recently, children chanted
o ampersand, instead of *zed*
at the alphabet's end. Things
were more open-ended then.

“ ”

You nestle speech within speech
caressing the talk of others.

You flit like fruit flies
over ripe bananas.

Or beckon like tadpoles
in a pond.

Ambidextrous remnants
of the numbers six and nine.

Enemy of the paraphrase
first cousin of the apostrophe.

When you appear, I relax,
for you signal respect.

I want to lie down
in your embrace.

Slim and
elegant, you streak
through the air trailing
endearments: my baby! my
sweetie! my jalapeño! You add bite,
make my heart burn, then you crank
up the volume, pound your fist, tell
me to watch my step, laugh your head
off when I trip, get indignant when
I complain, say you weren't born
yesterday, leap like a cougar
onto my back with a cry of
Take that! The only deterrent
to your thwack and bang,
you asshole you pinprick
of amazement, is to call
your exclamatory bluff
return you to the
land. Watch out!
I'm going to
turn you
upside
down
hand-
cuff
you
to a
tree

introduce
you to the
death of bravado
rhetoric and
mortality

( )

what is hidden
what is put aside

pigtail of the sentence
or most important thing said

sharp arc of embrace, the lines
a body follows as though drawn

hands cupped in prayer
breath held beneath hope

whole galaxies on the backs of knuckles
astonishment in the trough of tongues

widening curves of a lie
told, and once again, accepted

tumblehome of canoe
empty cradle rocking

a piece of sky caught in the legs
of a blue heron on its way home

forceps on a stubborn skull
the space a poem inhabits

tender lining of the moment
unearthed, uncatalogued

mouth of mountain, clutch
of woman, scratch of wound

where we are when we think
thoughts are real

where we are when we think
thoughts are just thinking

where we are when we think
we have all the time in the world

My black sun.
Hearth of the sentence.
Until you came along, words
FLOCKEDALLINCAPS, bunched
tight as passenger pigeons, wings
so close they blocked the sun.

A Greek librarian, well before Christ,
may have been the first to use you as a system
of points, sprinkled like raisins in pound cake,
settling here and there, above and below.
You are the wholes we dig ourselves into
when all has been said.

Derived from peri-odus, meaning
"around the path," you are more
philosophy than punctuation.
You complete the circuit of search
and find. Put a stop, a full stop, if only briefly,
to the traffic in our heads.
One more last chance.
These tiny cavities of prayer.

From the split second between sentences
to the pregnant time after a story or poem ends.
Open us to that consecrated space.
Open us up to the end.

?

O shaman of the sentence,
I love to watch you scythe through
the universe, cloaked like love
or death, in many disguises.

You're the private eye of punctuation.
Persistent as a two-year old drenched
with the why's of when,
the what's of now.
Crooked with hand to ear,
you wait and listen, poised above
an orb that could be a microbe,
a planet or the dark of the moon.
Or maybe you're a snake teetering
on a unicycle, juggling apples
of creation and interrogation.

What I like about you –
you're never satisfied.

Your mere presence raises the pitch
of our voices, as you dilate certainty
with your tremendous breath.
You never pretend to be the truth.
You know you're only half the story.
You stutter, repeat, insinuate,
hook yourself over barbed wire fences
and fling down barricades,
despite injuries you might sustain.

What I fear about you –
you're never satisfied.

You take prisoners, clip
wires to our tenderest parts,
jolt us until we are left
with a scimitar of scars.

So be careful, my Boolean baby,
my wild card, my glottal stop.
You are the logic we use to decide
what is true, what is false.
Even on those days when you're
tired as the rest of us, worn out
by asking the big questions,
fed up with bites of sound, words that buzz.
You're the only one who keeps us honest.
A soothsayer's staff picking our brains,
worming it out of us.

So please little one, don't cuff us to a chair.
Be kind in a persistent kind of way.
We need you more than any answer,
more than any truth, which is really
just one more question.

*

You used to have seven arms,
seven tear drops shooting from the centre,
seven heavens, seven seas, seven chakras,
seven virtues and seven sins.

Now that you have lost an arm,
you are relegated to rating movies or acting
as the queen of cover-up, landing splat in the
middle of words, a mere f***ing footnote.

Or you show up as a mysterious marker
of genetic makeup, that crazy-ass chromosome
belonging to one of the original gene pools,
before any mutations, humanity's random
spelling mistakes we pass on and on.

Snowflake of heredity, judge and jury,
daisy of uncertainty, or heavenly body of omission,
whatever your function, o asterisk,
you're still a star.

• • •

What a sibilant name you have
for the rapid backfire of omission,
the beginning of all sadness, all regret
for what might have been said,
what could have been meant.
Aren't you ashamed to be so vague?
Or is that your strategy?
The way you line up silences
like a row of fly specks, the trace
of tears, orbiting moons.
A necklace of black pearls
or the beginning of the fold-and-tear-here line.
Your succulent lips are irresistible
because you know, Ms. Ellipsis,
what we don't say often carries
more weight than what we do.

Such a load you carry on your triceps.
Is this your intention –
to leave room for the elastic
pause of hope, as you
trail off into absence
insisting we complete you?

O double pinhead
dagger of colonization
never direct
always explaining
leading us to expect
you've got the answer.
You dribble along
a tangle of intestine
ending up at:
yes: the rectum,
that final excretion
of all your verbiage
all your promises
all your excuses
about being too busy,
not having enough time,
you'll get to it tomorrow.
You lead us on and on
with your examples,
series of comments, lists
of things you have to do.
Why don't you just relax,
tip sideways, like
the eyes of crows:
come to an end.

;

You are the eyelash in my cream
of cauliflower soup, celadon worm
on a bed of steamed broccoli. Ugly,
ugly as a tick on a dog's belly.

Abrupt as coitus interruptus, maybe
even imperialist – exerting freedom
through force. You plant your flag
in the sentence's breeze as though
we don't know what country we're in
or who does what to whom.
You infatuate academics, put on
airs, tuxedos, hang your top hat
on the rack of imprecise thought.

You're supposed to signal a relationship
best left unexplained, hinting
"more will come, things
will get clearer." But really
you're nothing but a rusty hinge.
Though you do have an illustrious history.
Shakespeare peppered you
over his sonnets. Yet Samuel Beckett,
without any Jackson Pollock splatter
simply says:
"There I am then, (comma)
he leaves me, (comma)
he's in a hurry. (period)"

The one who tells panda jokes
loves you because you provide lift –

as though we must hover on semantic
thermals, inhabit the troposphere.
Granted, a master such as Virginia Woolf
can hold aloft her long sentences
with five of you and at least twelve commas.

The only solution may be to strike you
from our repertoire. Backspace,
delete, delete, let you go
from endangered to extinct –
the way of the ivory-billed woodpecker,
the eel grass limpet.

But easier said than done.
Why just last night, in a letter listing
skills I hoped would snare a job,
I used three of you.
There was no other way around it.
Which proves hostility can be set aside
and maybe, just maybe, there is hope
for a species such as ours.

So let's not wait
for deathbed regrets
to turn an awkward pause
into a full stop.

New, Used and Invented

Every language is an old-growth forest of the mind.

– Wade Davis

/

In the beginning God made a violent sweeping
gesture and said, Let there be a slash.
God saw that it was good

to line-break the heavens, to separate darkness
from light. So this God interrupted water
from water and called this sky.

There was evening and morning – the second day.
God created land/seas, plants/seeds, trees/fruit
and there was evening

and there was morning – the third day of punctuation.
Then sun/moon, stars/space/birds/land/wild animals
each according to its kind, livestock

and all the creatures according to their kinds.
Then God said, Let us make man in my image
and give him dominion

over the fish of the sea, the birds of the air, over
all the earth and the creatures that move
in my likeness.

And that's when God created ambiguity with a stroke
between God and man. For this slash
could mean

there is a choice. We can become
gods or mortals or we can join
the two.

And as one story goes, God took a slender curved
bone from the side of man to make
the human female

and commanded them both to fill the earth
and subdue it. And this
we have done.

And somehow we have fattened into nightmares
of so much choice that desire fastens to need
until we can't tell the difference.

Then the ninth month couples to its eleventh day,
and leaders preach fear, not dreams, insisting
we slash our own family's flesh.

And we create the rubble remains
of forests destroyed, the either/or
the godly gash

that binds us by how we choose
this mad little stroke to mean
as it flashes

between the conjoined twins of create/
destroy. So some days I despair
because beginnings go begging

and I just want this brave little stroke
to tilt, slight as a wink, as it creates
a place of breath, the space between
one line of poetry and the next.

>

you urge
buy more
do more
eat more
love more
work more
hate more
die more
and when two of you
get together you insist
much greater, so
much more

somehow we must
flip you horizontal

< >

I can't take my eyes off Stanley Kunitz's elbows.
I stare at them for the longest time on the back cover
before I open his last book, *The Wild Braid.*
Pale knobs, splashed with light, bent by the weight
of an aluminum bucket in each hand. Right hand
grips a walking stick not even touching ground
for hundred year old legs. I can't take my eyes
off Stanley Kunitz's elbows. They make me want
to weep. Their hinge of humerus, ulna and radius.
Joints gawky as the limbs of herons. His white head
rides at shoulder height. Shoulders wrinkle in folds
of burnt orange t-shirt. Ferns laden with spores
line the gravel path. A rose buds behind his back.

It's then I decide to focus on the backs of things.
On what has not been groomed, expected
or assumed, each glimpse a going closer,
a looking under. Stella d'oro petals thinned
by near frost, trying their best at fall blooms.
The backs of maple leaves beaded with rain
the way black velvet might display fire opals.
Celadon and raw umber instead of
blazing reds and oranges.

Later that morning I begin taking close-ups
of the backs of flowers. Stanley Kunitz's elbows
materialize as Japanese anemones, one single bloom
bent forward on a thin stem, flanked lower down
by a single bump of bud on either side.
How such tenderness of bone and bud spills
like late fall light, gesturing behind us
< while we're doing something else>
to all the wild beneaths.

You love to strip
down to fundamentals
no flashy adverbs
no fauning adjectives
just the slow, the small
the bare fact
the flat belly
and like till-less farming
where the earth
is not disturbed
except in the one spot
where a seed is planted
you control weed growth
you peel me down
to what I know is true –
that of all possible rhymes,
bless is the one
that fits you best.

High priestess
of codependence,
you cojoin those
not complete
on their own.

Addicted to drama
of the chaos-making kind,
you look for someone
to hitch yourself to.

You want intimacy,
but all you can do
is come within
spitting distance.

Then one day you
disappear from to-day
and to-morrow
and that's when
the present and future
begin their collapse.

‽

As a graphic, I find you distasteful as a butt crack on display. As a name, you sound like torture. Invented in the sixties by the head of an advertising agency, you haven't amounted to much, even though the Wall Street Journal proclaimed you exactly right for "Who forgot to put gas in the car‽"

Maybe you never caught on because we prefer the *bang! wow! zap!* of comic heroes to the confusion of one emotion superimposed on another.

Maybe it's easier to combine two meanings instead of two emotions. Humpty Dumpty says to Alice: "Well, *slithy* means *lithe* and *slimy* . . . You see it's like a portmanteau – there are two meanings packed up into one word."

Just as interrobang bundles *query* and *bang*. And *emoticon* packs up *emotion* and *icon*.

Who knew Nabokov conceived the most famous emoticon of them all when he answered the question "How do you rank yourself among living writers?"

I often think there should exist a special typographical sign for a smile — some sort of concave mark, a supine round bracket, which I would now like to trace in reply to your question.

©

Sea change in a circle,
you showed up with movable type,
staking claim to creative minds,
branding protection for a lifetime
plus fifty years.
Even the double helix
is subject to your little syndicate.
Corporations offer to copyright
our genes. If we're cloned,
we can sue.
More and more we ignore you.
No matter the work of a lifetime or an eon,
whatever is out there, we consider
ours for the taking,.
Perhaps the most lucrative
of signs, you may be just as much at risk
as blue-sided tree frogs, the black-spectacled
brush-finch, national economies.
I'm not sure if I'll miss
your little *c* of certainty,
your captive planet
of "mine, all mine."

—

What I love is your offer
of the unexpected,
your various names
even if I never know
which to use when.

em dash, en dash, figure dash, swung dash
three-quarter em dash, one-third em dash

You’ve been described, in your em dash
incarnation, as belonging to the “padded
and corseted aesthetic of Victorian typography.”
In your own defense you become staccato,
flamboyant, full of panache.

Hastily hotfoot it over here
you impetuous little stroke.
Link me some numbers, make
my life easy to memorize,
hyphenate me to June and July.
And while you’re at it, leave open
the gap after my birth date
for as long as you can.

^

Homophone
of the common
root vegetable

you germinate
where something
has been forgotten

tent of tenderness
stray diamond
of the sentence

without you
we wouldn't know
what we were missing.

•

You're here because I love
to say your name: interpunct.
Such authority in your plosives.
You used to be a small dot
centred between worlds,
forerunner of the inbetween.

My·little·middle·dot·
my·hovering·beauty·mark
salt·shaker·page·plaguer·
middle·child,
you serve as reminder
that fashion even affects
how we mark our speech
how we think of who we are
and what we might become.

⸮

You horny dissembler,
little question mark with
a hard on, signifier
of one thing said, another meant.
You croon "Beautiful day, isn't it,"
as rain pours from the gutters.
You snark, you zing.
You remove semantic security,
present the paradox of the insoluble,
the gap between what we wish were true
and what actually happens.

Some insist you are not
a rhetorical device, but a force
powerful enough to disrupt texts.
In Kierkegaard's words, you are
"infinite absolute negativity and
must swallow your own stomach."

You are the symbol of our struggle
to live with one thing on the surface
and something else
always lying
underneath.

You dingbats ring like
a cash register used to
or a bell still might.
You flit onto the page abrupt
as tropical fruit bats invading
a bunch of green bananas.
You deal heavy blows,
make us see stars, replace
middle letters of vulgar words
so no one is offended by what
everyone already thinks or says.
Then somehow you become
a silly person, a birdbrain.
Or a stand-in for that small object
whose name we've forgotten –
doohickey, gizmo, thingamabob.

You go to work when memory gaps.
When sense needs some nonsense.

At times you have meant
    muffin   male genitalia   money
    professional tramp   a woman
who is neither your sister nor your mother.

You jangle like hand-laid cast-metal type,
each letter the same height, each
with its own shoulder, foot, and face,
from a time when we used to handle
letters like precious stones.

You return us to the proto-alphabets
of country mailboxes with the flag up 📫
high-fiving hands ✋ fingers ☜ pointing
☝ e very ☟ which ☝ way ☟
thumbs up 👍 gestures of OK 👌
bombs with lit fuses 💣
airplanes at full-throttle ✈ ✈ ✈
a skull and crossbones ☠
sands of time
⌛
shifting, running out

You deserve your own space
on the keyboard, so I can touch
your bright tail of light, your dark
tadpole of tears, and caress the curve
between assumption and awareness
that tornadoes every human heart.

Shedding accusation, innuendo and distortion,
the full obama saunters on stage, slim
as an exclamation point, fires not just sound bites
but rounds of perfect prose more powerful
than a speeding bullet. Look! up on our screens –
the commander-in-chief of the English language.

Comfortable with complexity, you embrace
both black and white, but are defined by neither.
Know deep in your bones it's not about self,
but finding common ground, standing in the middle
of argument, addressing all points on the circle,
all that is dark within us, all that is light,
the light within the dark
and the dark within the light.

Is it any wonder the obama starts with the *o*
of ovation and ends with the *ah* of ecstasy,
literally a "standing outside oneself."

Because you know it all starts
and ends with the sound and sense
of the word, and it's up to us to discover
new ways to string these words together,
to stand beside ourselves and touch
the essence of others.

So for now, I'm going to let you
replace that fussbudget the semicolon,
interject you between two independent
and opposing clauses, suggesting
a third possibility and *yes*,
raise expectations that might not be met,
because what's important is how you manoeuvre
through our deepest structures, how you rest,
like winter's first snow, on each and every
dark branch, soft enveloping hard.

How you balance, in a time when
debt is measured in trillions,
like a lone tai chi master.

How you perch plump as a thrush,
singing your song twice over.
Once for the dark ☯ once for the light.

❄

"Used at the end of a unique familial phrase–that is, any sequence of words that has never, in the history of our family life, been assembled as such. For example, "I didn't die in the Holocaust, but all of my siblings did, so where does that leave me? ❄*" Or, "My heart is no good, and I'm afraid of dying, and I'm also afraid of saying I love you*❄*"*

– Jonathan Safran Foer,
"A Primer for the Punctuation of Heart Disease"

Widely believed no two alike,
like Tolstoy's unhappy families,
these supercooled droplets
precipitate siblings of truth

(you're the main course,
and I'm just a side dish ❄)

but if such weather patterns
are observed, it is possible
snowflakes may indicate what
needs to be said, what needs
to be done, or undone, offer
a new forecast for familial
thunder snows, because despite
this lattice of sleet, I love you,
even though sometimes I'm afraid
of what we'll both do
with this love ❄

{ }

Here is the space
that houses the unspoken.

You know those words.
You have rehearsed them
over and over, and now
you have a place
to shelter them,
away from the light,
biding your time
until you are ready
to open their intricately
carved doors.

~

In math you
signal negation,
in pronunciation
you turn ñasal,
in front of a number,
you approximate.
          But what if,
my emphatic eyebrow
my cowlick, handlebar
mustache, wave without end,
what if I don't want you
to measure or nullify
but to hum a tune,
slowly
     turning
               in 3/4 time
come
come a-waltzing,
my tilde, with me.

You come from the days
when we still struck mechanical keys
that put real ink on real paper,
when underlining required many strokes
and letters had force and weight.
When a poem on a sheet of paper
circled the platen, calling out
as we passed it on the way to the fridge.

You come from a time when ink could
smudge, when a fast typing speed
guaranteed a job and courier
was the standard typeface.
When heavy strokes on keys
cut alphabet shaped holes.
When the shift key actually
moved something.

When each line-break required
a flick of the wrist and a pause
while the carriage moved itself
to the left and pushed the paper
up one line.

You used to draw attention
to the titles of things, but now
your bunk buddy the hyphen
gets more job offers.
                                        Your main function,
my lanky low line, seems to be
to require us to fill in
our expiration date.

ΔΔ

I'm weary with invention cannot find the strength to reject an idea for punctuation: two small triangles a pair of pricked-up ears.

– Anne Szumigalski, from "Fennec,"
On Glassy Wings: Poems New & Selected

I'm weary with invention
listen only to the alphabet
of robin and red tailed fox

cannot find the strength
to sleep or walk through
the muds of spring

reject an idea for punctuation hourly,
every minute I'm marked
by exclamations

two small triangles of leaf
jot down elegies to the wind

a pair of pricked-up ears,
the peek and tut
of robins defending.

[}

Here is where you place
what you would have done
between the square bracket
of *if* and the curly bracket
of *only*

between the hard wall of
        [*why*
and the bird in flight
                    } *because.*

Here is where we sit
when we wish
we could take back
harsh words
        an unkind gesture.

I know this space.
I have sat here often.

¡

whisper into my hand
murmur sweet somethings
short stubby words like lick
and love, bristle me
with whiskers.

whisper into my ear
let me unhear you
lie beside me dense
as ocean, mumble me
some mist

whisper into my hair
legendary moans
soft trusting sounds
of coddle and coo

whisper into my mouth
hush me, breathe me
your secrets and I promise
to keep them close
as my next breath

spritz the air with foreground
flutter as clouds ghost the tips
of spruce and cedar

unexclaim me.

Your five fingers stand
for the hand of Miriam,
hiding her brother Moses,
and the hand of Fatima,
daughter of Mohammed,
the five books of the Torah,
the Five Pillars of Islam,
Five People of the Cloak.

You avert the evil eye,
offer a handful of protection.

Let's hope you will rise
above words of discord,
beyond vendettas exacting
blood revenge and once again,
save brothers, honour daughters,
create that perfect fifth,
the most consonant of harmonies.

Come on, gimme five.

Follow this scatter of marks
down a path beaten by use,
along the old logging road
that parallels the field.
If you are still, you might even
glimpse deer in the distance,
pause and take comfort
in evidence of the wild.

Bend to study these prints in the snow.
Notice how like phalluses they are.
Nothing like the drawings in field guides:
blackened lungs, butterfly wings
mounted and framed.
Look at their ruffled track of
twin minarets, opposing thumbs,
the perked ears of rabbits.
No bigger than the clamps
tightening your snow shoes,
they freckle the path
with black tears on the run.

Consider what would happen
if you inserted these tracks
in your cultivated prose.
Embed them next to oversized
or one-size-fits-all thoughts,
where human is still held
separate from nature.
This may be one way to proceed,
as the doe are pregnant now
and will give birth in the spring.

Tzetel - Yiddish for a small scrap
of paper on which you write a prayer.

Little notebook, someone said.
That's what Zetlin means.

With the field as notebook
and breath as prayer

I want to walk through the field,
walk until the word field is gone.

Notes

@ In languages other than English, names for the @ range from animals (snail, worm, little dog) to body parts (elephant's trunk, monkey's tail, cat's foot, pig's ear) to food (rollmops herring, strudel, cinnamon roll). See also www.robertfulford.com/AtSymbol2.html.

& At the beginning of the 19th century, this symbol was taught as the 27th letter of the alphabet, but it didn't have a name. Schoolchildren ended the chanting of their ABCs with "and, per se, and" which meant "&, which means 'and.'" This phrase eventually slurred into ampersand.

– Robert Bringhurst described the dash as belonging to the "padded and corseted aesthetic of Victorian typography."

; Warning: some violence occurred in the making of this poem. Three semicolons were bruised, one sustained a broken limb and another was throttled and left in the margins.

"The semicolon is ugly, ugly as a tick on a dog's belly, I pinch them out of my prose." – attributed to Donald Barthelme.

"If you really want to hurt your parents . . . the least you can do is go into the arts. But do not use semicolons. They are transvestite hermaphrodites, standing for absolutely nothing. All they do is show you've been to college." – Kurt Vonnegut

"the one who tells panda jokes" is Lynne Truss, author of *Eats, Shoots & Leaves: The Zero Tolerance Approach to Punctuation.*

Grave Sweeping Day
A found poem courtesy of Zappha Barfoot.

Field Work
"The fields are impatient/ for someone to believe in them." was inspired by Dennis Lee's line "the fields wait patiently as though someone believed in them," from "400: Coming Home," *Nightwatch: New & Selected Poems* 1968-1996. McClelland & Stewart.

Acknowledgements

A handful of these poems was published in *The Thing With Feathers* (BuschekBooks), several were broadcast on CBC radio, and the ‘?’ and ‘;’ were hand printed as broadsheets by Fred Turner. A selection of these poems was short listed for the 2009 CBC Literary Awards. ‘< >’ was short listed for the 2009 Arc Poem of the Year. A version of the '☯’ was recorded for the CD “Hear Now,” a fundraising project for Youth Literacy, available from www.sgbyouthliteracy.org. All photos are by the author, except the aerial photos, taken by Telfer Wegg.

Thanks to Don McKay, who first read some of these poems at the Banff Writing Studio in 2001, and understood, perhaps better than I did, what I was aiming for – combining poems, images and site specific work. Many years later, Don gave me the idea for a separate section incorporating the field photos and describing the process of creating the punctuation field. I’m indebted to Allen Briesmaster, who helped me edit an earlier version of the manuscript and to my friend and thoughtful reader, Judy Lowry. Special thanks to Black Moss editors Susie Heinrichs and Jessica Minervini, both of whom challenged me and helped find the shape of the book. Thanks to Marty Gervais for believing in this collection of poems and for all that he has done for poetry. And as always, thanks to my husband, Don Holman, for his generous and constant support.

Elizabeth Zetlin resides in Traverston, Ontario, with her husband Don Holman. She is an award winning poet, visual artist and filmmaker. Liz was Owen Sound's inaugural Poet Laureate and is currently artistic director of the Words Aloud Spoken Word & Storytelling Festival held in Durham, Ontario.